INDECENT WHIPPING.

I HAVE read with much pleasure your manly and outspoken remarks on the subject of "Indecent Whipping of Girls." I would every parent did the same, and there would soon be an end to the very serious mischief. Perhaps you may think this letter worthy of insertion as tending to show that this evil is not an imaginary one, and though I approach it with loathing and disgust, I do so in the hope that my own experience of this mode of punishment in girls' schools may prove a warning to others.

About six months ago I sent my only daughter, aged fourteen, to a highly respectable middle-class school in one of the midland counties. Being an active, high-spirited girl, and quite unused to the strict discipline and control of boarding school life, she unwittingly, by some childish irregularity, offended the head mistress. She was sent for, awarded an imposition, admonished, and told that the next offence would entail a whipping. Two or three days after this my daughter again incurred Miss B ——'s displeasure, and this is what happened : She was taken upstairs and arrayed in a punishment dress—i.e., a long calico garment, resembling a night-dress—conducted to the dining-hall, and then and there stripped naked in the presence of the whole school, and flogged by the gardener, being held meanwhile by two of the day-masters. The poor child's shrieks and prayers for mercy were disregarded, and the most brutal punishment administered by a man's strong right hand, with a birch-rod, continued. Several eye-witnesses state that when she was released, after receiving between fifteen and twenty cuts, she would have fallen to the floor fainting almost, but was caught in the arms of a bystander. Needless to say, on this outrage reaching my ears, I had her immediately removed, and only my dread of seeing the thing reported in the public newspapers prevented my immediately instituting legal proceedings I think, Sir, I have said enough to endorse the truth of your remarks, and need only add that, if by your powerful pen you can mitigate, expose, or eradicate this crying disgrace to our girls' schools, you will earn the lasting gratitude of many such as your obedient servant,

A PARENT.

Some of your correspondents seem to doubt that young women are publicly whipped in boarding schools. Let me confirm the statements of many ladies who have addressed you on this subject, and inform you that at the school at which I was a pupil for two years whippings were regularly inflicted, and on the bare flesh. Of course these were for serious breaches of the school regulations only, and were somewhat frequent. I cannot conceal from myself now the fact that the teachers felt some pleasure in exposing the persons of their pupils, and then thrashing them; but that parents should wilfully blind themselves to the existence of these practices is much to be deplored. On several occasions masters were present at these whippings, and there was no mistaking the expression on their faces while the castigation was in course of infliction. Whenever parents arrange for the stay of their daughters at boarding schools, they should enquire whether indecent whipping is practised, and then act accordingly. For men to be present is, of course, exceptional; but I think that any system of punishment which necessitates the removal of clothing, and, consequently, the exhibition of the naked person, even to a woman, is highly indecent and improper. Some of your correspondents seem to think it worse when the girl is bigly built and well developed. In my opinion it is no different when the pupil is thin and of small proportions. The indecency is just the same, and I hope the correspondence you are publishing will put a stop to the indecent whippings.

A LATE BOARDING SCHOOL PUPIL.

As regards the whipping of girls at school, I think there is in some cases far too much of it, and in other cases far too little. I will relate an instance that came under my own knowledge when teaching in the schools at which they occurred. One day, in March last, at a school conducted by a foreign lady, a girl of about eighteen years of age, who was in my class, so far misconducted herself in refusing to obey my orders, that I was obliged to report the matter to Miss ——, who at once told the girl she must be whipped, and sent her for the birch-rod used for the purpose. I, of course, did not expect this, nor did I think, when I had heard it, that the whipping would be inflicted in my class-room, but I was mistaken. The girl returned in a short time with the birch, and appeared as if she were expecting Miss —— to leave the room with her, but not so. The woman (I cannot call her a lady) locked the door, and put the key in her pocket, telling her victim—a stout girl of ladylike appearance—to prepare for whipping. The girl begged to be allowed to go to another room, and I, of course, requested to be allowed to leave, but Miss —— would not allow it, nor could I induce her to surrender the key. Assisted by two other girls, who were too much afraid to refuse, she removed the girls dress, stays, and petticoats, leaving nothing upon her but the last two garments. She then forced her down upon a form, face downwards, and told her she should lie so till she asked for twenty strokes. The poor girl must have nearly fainted with fright, but the shame of her nude condition soon induced her to ask for the punishment to be inflicted. When it was over she was allowed to remain where she was for some time longer, "to show her," as Miss —— said, "her duty." I have never seen a female in so shameful a position, and I contend that nothing could well be more indecent than this. I left the school soon after, as did also the poor girl who was whipped. I am afraid I have trespassed on your space too much to continue longer now.

MONITOR.

I feel quite sure that the majority of your readers and the public at large have little conception of the terribly cruel whippings that are inflicted in schools on the Continent. I was engaged as a governess in a very expensive one near Paris, and was not altogether averse to corporal chastisement for serious offences properly administered. In the establishment I refer to, however, the young ladies were, for the slightest faults, whipped most mercilessly. I have frequently seen young women of eighteen and nineteen years of age receive twenty cuts with the birch, vigorously applied to their bare persons, for the removal of their drawers was always insisted upon, simply for speaking English during prohibited hours, and for serious offences it was not unusual for two, three, or even four dozen strokes to be given, and as a refinement of cruelty a girl was often ordered to receive her punishment by instalments of, say four, six, or eight strokes each day for a week. The state of the poor creature's person towards the end of the punishment (?) was truly shocking. In nearly every whipping the blood was brought, and the rods were always steeped in brine before use.

The Martinet, an instrument very generally used for correction, was also applied very severely. It consists of a handle, to which are attached twelve or more leather thongs. It does not cut the flesh like the rod, but leaves it discoloured with livid weals. This was sometimes applied to the back and shoulders of the culprit, and was usually given when the lower part of the poor girl's person was too sore from birching to bear another whipping, but who had unfortunately transgressed some of the numerous rules for which a whipping is ordered.

I could not remain and witness these frequent and barbarous punishments, so left at the termination of my first term. I can assure you that the above account is not an exaggeration of what transpires in very many schools; and in convent schools, I have heard, and quite believe, the unhappy inmates are flogged without mercy or decency. I may add that, in my opinion, a girl can be made to feel the birch with her drawers on, and that to remove them, unless for the most serious offences, is a cruel addition to the suffering the rod produces.   M. A. F.

Permit me, as a schoolmistress of over thirty years' experience, to offer a few remarks on this subject.

No one who has had anything to do with the management and education of children can doubt the necessity of using the rod. Now nature has provided one place where, more especially in the case of girls, without danger to health or appearance, a sound whipping can be applied, and to render it efficacious, it must be upon the bare person. Whether in the case of boys or girls, I can see nothing indecent in this, if it be inflicted by teachers of their own sexes.

My plan was—for ordinary offences I ordered the young lady to come to my bed-room at night when she was prepared for bed, and privately whipped her. For graver faults I summoned the rest of her class to witness it, and for very bad conduct I whipped the culprit publicly before the whole school in one of the largest bed-rooms. I used a birch-rod of moderate size, and had a block, much like that used at Eton, for young ladies to kneel across. She was fastened to it by one strap around her waist, and another just below the knees, If any struggle or resisting took place, I doubled the number of strokes.

Now let me relate an experience. In my school there were two large bed-rooms under the care of a governess, and the rest of the girls slept, by five or six, in smaller rooms, in each of which the eldest young lady was responsible. On one occasion one of the gove nesses reported to me a most indecent and improper conversation she had heard carried on in one of these bed-rooms, occupied by Miss S., aged seventeen, Miss H., sixteen, and three younger girls of fourteen, thirteen, and twelve years respectively. I sent for the young ladies, informed them of the complaint, and directed them to come to my room that night to receive a whipping. Miss S. and Miss H. objected, but I told them if they did not come I should expel them next morning.

The six young ladies having undressed to their shoes and chemises, and having put on their dressing-gowns. came to my room, where the under mistresses were assembled. Each of them, beginning with the youngest, removed her dressing-gown, and laid herself on the block. Her chemise was raised, and one of the under mistresses, under my supervision, administered to the two youngest four strokes, and to the two next six strokes. Miss H. received ten strokes, and on rising from her knees burst into tears. Miss S., without even changing colour, knelt down. The governess held up her clothing and I gave her twelve sharp cuts with a larger birch. Retaining her composure with an effort, she rose, and all retired.

I then directed one of the under mistresses to sleep in the room, as my suspicions had been aroused. In a fortnight she informed me that conversation of the filthiest type was indulged in, and most disgusting practices carried on. One especially she had discovered of which all the young ladies were guilty, Miss S.'s conduct in particular being of the worst description. I sent for the six girls, told them I should severely whip the four younger, and that next mornig Miss S. and Miss H. should be expelled. They both fell on their knees, and implored me not to do that, but to give them any other punishment. At last I consented, and directed them to attend as before that evening. I then ordered the head girl in every room to be present at the punishment. The mistress had told me that Miss S. had laughed at her former whipping, but that Miss H. seemed to have felt it acutely.

The girls attended. The four younger ones received twelve strokes each, the last four cuts in each case producing cries and screams. Miss H. then knelt down. I informed her she should receive fifteen strokes, eight then, and seven after Miss S. had received hers Her chemise was fastened up at her shoulders, and the most vigourous mistress wielded the rod. Miss H. sobbed and cried as the sixth, seventh, and eighth stroke fell. Then leaving her in the same position, I called Miss S. forward, strapped her firmly to a frame at the foot of my bed, and as soon as she was thus firmly secured standing up, one of the mistresses fastened up her chemise round her neck, leaving her person below the shoulders bare. I having announced her punishment twenty strokes, took up a light riding whip, and administered a sharp cut just below the shoulder blades. Miss S. made desperate efforts to retain her composure, but at the eighth stroke it failed, and as I counted twelve, thirteen, and fourteen, she fairly yelled with pain. I then took up the birch-rod, and gave the other seven cuts to Miss H., who was then suffered to rise, sobbing and crying like a child. Her person had assumed a deep pink colour, and she fairly stamped on the ground, so much did she smart.

Returning to Miss S., whose entreaties to let her off I disregarded, I gave her the other six cuts on the lower part of her back, which up to that I had left untouched. I administered them with all the strength I could, and each one of them produced a deep purple mark, and was received with shrieks and sobs.

No doubt this was a terrible punishment, but it was weeks ere Miss H. or Miss S. ceased to feel its effects, and the lesson was never forgotten. From that night I never had any indelicate language to complain of. And note the result. Miss H. personally thanked me for her whipping some years afterwards. And a few years ago, after I had given up my school, Miss S. wrote to express her regret I was no longer able to take pupils, as she was then happily married, and wished to find a school for her little girl. She concluded by saying, "I can never thank you enough for that flogging. It cured me of a most abominable vice, and to your kind severity I owe all my present happiness."   W. G.

One of your correspondents, "An Old Boy," seems to imply that women are actuated by improper motives when flogging boys of sixteen or seventeen years of age. At least, he says that a woman, who must have been old enough to have been his mother (or she would not have been in the responsible position of housekeeper in a good school), ought not to have been allowed to place him across her knees and slap him like a child, as he thinks it conducive to immorality. If he thinks it is on the woman's side, I, as a woman, and the mother of a family, beg to differ with him, as the most objectionable time in a boy's life is at the foolish and awkward age of from sixteen to nineteen years, and when a childish punishment is of the most service. Far from a woman of mature years being actuated by bad motives in chastising a boy of sixteen or seventeen, I think it would and does excite only a feeling of disgust in a properly regulated mind that the childish faults of the would-be young man should require so childish a remedy. I have boys of my own, and should be pleased if they were away from home and my own discipline if a sensible, motherly woman should give them a good, old-fashioned slapping when overstepping the bounds of propriety. The vast amount of self-esteem, self-confidence, and boundless impudence of lads between sixteen and eighteen years of age is very disgusting to a woman of sense, and the best way to check it is to impose a punishment suitable to a badly behaved child and sufficiently ridiculous to shame, and this can be done and will be felt more acutely by the youth when inflicted in the old style across the knees of a matronly sensible woman.

AN OLD GIRL.

As you will see by the note accompanying this I am staying in France at the establishment of Madame ———. I may at once tell you that the administration of bodily punishment to the pupils is of frequent occurence. Of this I do not for one moment complain as I consider the whipping of girls to be absolutely necessary to keep them in subjection, all other modes of punishment being in my own idea mere child's play and only calculated to excite ridicule in the pupil's breast. At all events, they did in mine so there I can speak from experience. But what I do consider most shameful is the degredation and shame to which I was exposed whilst being punished for an offence of which I will not now speak. Is it right that a girl—I might almost say a woman—should be forcibly whipped in the presence of a man? Even as I write I blush with shame to think of the indignities put upon me by Madame ———, and shall never as long as I live forget them. I dare not give you the details of the shameful proceeding, but it will suffice if I tell you that I was treated in the manner that a mere child would have been, and this in the presence of a man. And I, Sir, am now seventeen years of age and consider that it was most wrong and cruel of Madame to cause me to be whipped in an almost nude condition in the presence of a common man. I am writing this as a warning to all mothers to be careful in making inquiries ere they place their daughters in a school where such indignities are perpetrated as those of which I was a victim. Sincerely trusting that you will not put my name to this letter.—Believe me, yours sincerely,

---

Upon reading the letter with reference to whipping addressed to you by the young lady from France, allow me to say that I do not consider it is in the slightest degree exaggerated. I well remember sending my two daughters, aged respectively thirteen and fifteen, to a school where in answer to my enquiries, I was positively assured that corporal punishment in that establishment was not tolerated

You may judge of my surprise and indignation when, upon my girls returning home for their holidays, one of the (the younger) informed me, after some hesitation, that she had been publicly whipped, also her elder sister. Asked what she meant by "publicly whipped" she refused to tell me, and no threats or persuasion of mine could elicit details from her. So taking my other daughter into my confidence, she informed me, after a great deal of natural reluctance, that both she and her sister had been twice whipped for a very trivial offence in presence of the music master and his nephew. As the music master was a married man of over sixty years of age, I will pass that over, but for two young girls to be whipped upon their naked persons in the presence of a young man of about twenty-five is too much, and is to my mind disgusting. I need hardly tell you that my daughters were removed from that school, and for the future taught at home.

I have no objection, should you desire it, to furnish you in confidence with the name and locality of the school, but I must request you not to publish my name in connection with this letter. In conclusion I ask you, can no means be found to put an end to these disgusting practices in so-called respectable "seminaries" for young ladies? I should like to have the experiences of other mothers with regard to this question, as I cannot believe that this indecent whipping is of rare occurence.

AN INDIGNANT MOTHER.

Although I am not in favour of whipping girls above the age of thirteen, I fail to see how the term "indecent" can be applied to an old-fashioned punishment for girls under age. Those who have the custody of children know full well how wilful and disobedient they can be at times, and how necessary it is to have some means at hand to check their bad behaviour. To accomplish this no other punishment is so effectual or so harmless as a good hearty spanking. This plan is very much in favour in many families, even at the present day, and I have heard many parents remark that so much is it dreaded by young girls that sometimes the mere threat of inflicting it has the desired effect of compelling obedience. I do not believe in severity ; it is in my opinion quite needless, and I feel sure that if governesses at school would adopt the plan in private for young girls there would be no need whatever to discuss their bad conduct. There must be a certain amount of uncovering, and I think the party administering the chastisement should herself unfasten and lower the girls' drawers after she is placed over the knee. This adds to the feeling of shame produced, and convinces the child that there is an authority which it would be well for her not to set at nought.

ONE IN FAVOUR OF THE OLD STYLE.

I do not think any of your correspondents have drawn attention to the fact that girls while under punishment at schools are often left exposed an unnecessary length of time in order to gratify the vile propensities of brutal onlookers, both male and female. I quite agree that it is almost an impossibility to maintain discipline in schools without some kind of punishment, but that this punishment should be contrived so as to afford gratification to some beasts is a disgrace to our educational system and to the law which permits it. I hope you will go on exposing the vile proceedings in boarding schools, till some improvement is effected. I buy two dozen copies of your paper weekly and distribute them far and wide among parents who have daughters likely to go to boarding schools, and if some of your readers were to follow my example, we should be able to effect something tangible in a very short time.—G.W.L.

I cannot speak on this subject with reference to English schools, but my experience in Continental ones has convinced me that the birch is used far too freely and too severely abroad. I will give you an instance from a school in Paris, where I had the misfortune to be engaged about two months. One of the girls had committed a rather serious offence against the rules of the establishment, and had been told she would be whipped. She was a fair delicate girl, and was much frightened at the sentence; but she was hurried off to bed, where she remained till about four o'clock, when the lessons for the day were finished. The whole school was then assembled in the dining room, and the poor girl was brought down in her dressing gown. This was taken off by two maids, and she was then laid on her face on a raised sofa, while the mistress discoursed upon the enormity of her offence. Her nightdress was then pulled over her head, leaving the whole of her person exposed, and herself in a fainting condition, while her legs and arms were held by the maids. She then received no less than thirty strokes, each one leaving its mark on her thin white skin, and at the twentieth the lower part of her back and her thighs were bleeding profusely. At the end of the punishment she was literally carried off to bed. I think, Sir, you will agree with me that the above was a truly revolting exhibition, and I showed my disgust at it by sending in my resignation at once.

I certainly think that for serious offences girls should be birched, but I think that when it is necessary it should be inflicted when the girl is in bed, and in privacy, as the girl's person can then be bared, and the punishment inflicted in a much shorter space of time than is the case when the girl has to be stripped of her every-day garments. Hoping that the discussion taking place in your valuable journal may bring about a revolution in this mode of punishment.

M. S.

I am glad to have an opportunity of exposing a case of whipping which took place at a West-End school. My daughter, a well-grown girl of fifteen, was behind-hand with her French exercise, and was reported by the French master to the lady superintendent. A message was sent to her to remain after school, which she did, expecting a reprimand and extra lessons, which, no doubt, she well deserved. Imagine her surprise when, after school, she and the whole class, some seventeen or eighteen girls, were called to the head mistress' study, and she was then told to " prepare for punishment." So taken aback was she that she did not know what to do, and on the mistress touching a bell, two stout maids came in and stripped the poor girl to her chemise, also removing her drawers. She was then told to kneel down and lean over a chair, and while held in that position, received twelve hard and sharp cuts with a long birch-rod. An eye-witness, one of her fellow pupils, told me,

" It was sickening to see. The girl cried and begged for mercy, and writhed so at each stroke that the maids could hardly hold her in a position to receive the punishment from the hands of the mistress. When it was over she ran about the room like a mad thing, crying for her mother, and was some ten minutes before she could be dressed and sent away." I need hardly say she did not return to school, and it was some days before the cruel marks of the birch disappeared from her skin. One of the girls looking on fainted, others laughed, some cried. Such is the difference of girls' nature. Punishment may be needed, but surely not such public disgrace as this.

AN INDIGNANT MOTHER.

I am a young girl not long home from school, and my brother has shown me some letters in your paper on the subject of school punishments, and has also asked me to write to you. While at school I would have aided any movement to put an end to birching, but now I must honestly say I think a good whipping is occasionally very necessary and useful. I was naturally very idle, and was cured, or at all events, stimulated to work by a couple of sound whippings—one in private and one in the class-room—in neither could I see anything so indecent or so dreadfully disgusting as some of your correspondents profess to do. They were simply very, very painful and unpleasant experiences, which nobody would like to renew. There was no elaborate undressing or preparation. In the first instance I was taken upstairs by my teacher to the principal's room—complaint and lecture once made and given and in the end the teacher drew me towards her, and stooping over me, gathered up my clothes behind, and rendered me partially bare, holding me so while madame gave me nine or ten stinging stripes. I mended my ways, but relapsing after a little, although warned, I was called up for punishment before my schoolfellows. It was a trying moment and long dwelt in my memory, and I believe the dread of having to go through such an ordeal again made me diligent. I had to kneel on the seat of a detached desk at the top of the room, my body resting across the upper portion. A teacher stood on either side of me, and after turning up my clothes and letting down all my other underclothing as far as they would go, they held me in position. These preliminaries did not occupy three minutes ; and madame, with a long, slender rod of nine switches, gave me twelve or fifteen strokes, not hastily, but with a pause between each to give it full effect. I tried to count the strokes but failed after the first few. The pain was so great, causing me to feel as if I was being pricked with red hot needles. Yet, when all was over, there was no blood drawn, as some of your correspondents describe, nor any of the very shocking appearances they allude to. The marking was much less than I could have expected, and next night there was scarcely a trace of it. There was no laughing or ugly remarks among the girls ; I met nothing but sympathy and kindness all round, and I am convinced the only feeling a public whipping (and they were few) created was one of general horror.

Girls very often have favourite vices, which, if allowed to grow, become confirmed failings. Madame, who was always good, kind and just, seemed in some mysterious manner always to alight on these failings. If she could cure them by honesty and advice, well and good, if not the rod was invoked, but she never whipped in passion or unjustly. I have known many girls who were reformed, it might be after the first or it might be after the fourth whipping, but there was no use in resisting. I only know one instance where the rod did not win in the end. ALICE.

I quite agree with the majority of your correspondents that whipping in schools, as now practised, is an unmixed evil. That immoral habits arise out of it I am assured. It is perhaps at preparatory schools, attended by boys and girls up to the age of twelve and fourteen, that children are more freely whipped than at other institutions. Boys at fourteen, now-a-days, know a great deal more about the relations of the sexes than it is advisable they should, and the evil, therefore, of exposing a girl, and whipping her before a lad of that age, need not be commented upon. I wish that some horrible habits engendered among school boys could be written of in a newspaper; but it is my opinion that by abolishing indecent whipping, you remove the cause of many filthy habits. SCRUTTON,

There seems a wonderful diversity of opinion upon a theme which in reality admits of but one conclusion, especially where girls are concerned. It is simply revolting to entertain, even for a moment, the idea that the so-called "weaker sex" can only be "trained in the way they sdould go" by being indecently and disgustingly exposed to punishment which, to say the least, is but a remnant of the age of barbarism. No expression can be strong enough, no expletive harsh enough in which to condemn such a procedure. Are we retrograding in the nineteenth century? Are we becoming brutalised instead of civilised? Is it necessary to use the lash in the training of our daughters, the future mothers of brave heroes, of learned and enlightened men, of clever statesmen, of the thousand and one grades which make up the population of Briton's mighty Empire? No! Indeed anyone with a grain of decency, with a little refinement, would shudder at the idea of whipping even a little girl, much less a young woman, or one that is just unfolding the lovely blossoms of girlhood, which by-and-bye develop into the still lovlier charm of holy womanhood. A mother's curse upon those who advocate the horrid system of whipping, no matter for what heinous offence. Are people who are paid for training children to experience no trouble in fitting and beautifying the natural clay into some useful and ornamental form? If the teachers are incapable, are the pupils to suffer? There are hundreds of principals of schools who are as much fitted to have the charge of young girls as the charges themselves, the consequence is that pupil and teacher clash, and no one knows the cause. A teacher must be create, not manufactured. The mere possession of a government certificate and a knowledge of all the "logics" does not constitute a teacher. A woman who undertakes to train an English girl should be thoroughly womanly; she should possess a full knowledge of human nature, she should be able to bear with the faults and foibles of girlhood, and above all, she should govern by kindness, her only weapon a loving and sympathetic heart. She would thus never require rod or whip to bring her pupils to submission. They would fear to offend, not because of punishment, but the wish to please, the wish to gain the word of approval, the kindly smile would have more effect in gaining submission than all the modes of punishment ever invented. Now and then if a refractory one turned up, the best example to make of her would be to divide her from her fellows, and by thus setting a mark upon her, touch her self-respect, and if that failed expel her. Be sure that if a girl will not submit without being whipped, she is a "bad lot" and even the whipping will not influence her for good. Therefore nothing can be gained by taking part in such scenes as have been so painfully described in former issues of your journal "Mothers of England," to arms, and if no other means are possible, invoke the aid and strength of the laws of your country. Do not allow your daughters to be degraded to the level of the brute creation, foster the potent charm of modesty in your offspring, and do away with one fell swoop the rankling canker of "Indecent Whipping." A BRITISH MATRON.

I venture to think that it is an error to suppose that whipping is an effectual punishment. I believe any boy would rather be whipped and have done with it, than be kept in on a half holiday and lose his cricket. As for girls, I should feel sure that they would consider extra lessons and deprivation of luxuries at meals worse punishments than a whipping. If this is true, surely the punishment of whipping should be given up, for if it is not feared, how can it avail? If it is supposed that the disgrace is dreaded, I am sure no boy cares for that or feels any—and I doubt if any girl does either; but a separate seat in class and at meals may be made a stool of shame and repentance, and thus punishment given which is likely to be useful, whereas I believe whipping never is, because it is not dreaded nor does it deprive the pupil of playtime or of anything for which he or she cares. JAMES HOPTON.

THE BIRCH.

By H. BAKER.

The Editor of this pamphlet does not necessarily identify himself with Mr. Baker's views.

CHAPTER I.

INTRODUCTION.

THAT the whip and the birch are very ancient institutions is evidenced by the fact that, in the palmy days of ancient Rome, the Vestal Virgins who were entrusted to keep watch over the sacred fires in the Temple, and replenish them with fuel lest they should go out, if they failed in their duty, and allowed these fires to become extinguished, were led by a priest to a dark room, where, covered with a thin veil, they were whipped by him for their offence. The Vestal Urbinia was so whipped, and afterwards led in procession through the streets of Rome.

The practice of flagellation certainly has antiquity in its favour, but in considering a question in these days, we do not ask, How long has any institution or any thing existed? but, Is it good? The saints adopted this method of atoning for their sins. Peter the Hermit, Rodolph, and Dominic Loricatus used to correct themselves with rods and birches. The last-named always carried his scourges with him, and flogged himself regularly at bed-time. In ancient Greece and Rome, the whipping of slaves was much in vogue. To such a pitch, indeed, did this practice attain in Rome that some of the Emperors made laws for the purpose of checking it. By these laws it was enacted that any Roman who should intentionally kill a slave should suffer banishment, and any lady who caused a slave to be whipped to death, suffering the death to take place within three days after the infliction, was liable to excommunication for at least five years.

There are many anecdotes related concerning the use of the discipline; and some, indeed, of them are more amusing than otherwise, although they lead one to pity the poor weak-minded creatures who would allow their spiritual directors so blindly to tyrannise

over them. The following is a specimen of one of these anecdots :—
The widow of a Landgrave of Hesse, and Thuringia Elizabeth,
daughter of King Andreas II. of Hungary, suffered much from the
severity of her confessor, Conrad of Marburg. He was suspected of
being the lover of the princess, and when one of her friends, Schenk
von Argula, hinted at the rumour, she folded back a part of her
dress, saying, "You may see the kind of love this holy man bears to
me and I to him." Her skin was torn and bleeding from a severe
whipping she had just had for a trifling disobedience.

It was, perhaps, scarcely conducive to public morality that flogging
was, during the dark, middle ages, so much a part and parcel of
every civilised state. It was a poor kind of civilisation which pos-
sessed the world six hundred years ago, but as it was not absolute
barbarism which reigned supreme, that age is entitled to be desig-
nated civilised. Wherever there was chivalry there was civilisation,
and the most obstinate expounders of the civil and religious darkness
and thraldom of the middle ages cannot but admit that the great and
noble attribute of chivalry at that period held wide possession over
the minds and the hearts of the bodies of knights and others who had
taken vows to devote their energies to the delivery of the oppressed,
and the comforting of the afflicted.

It would occupy too much space to relate anything pretending to
be a history of the disciplinary mortifications which gained ground
at this period. Early in the thirteenth century a scare called "The
Flagellants" made its appearance in Italy. There was a sort of
epidemic of superstition. They believed themselves to be dreadfully
wicked, and that the only acceptable proof of their contrition lay in
scourgings. One account says : "Noble as well as ignoble persons,
young and old, even children five years old, would go naked about
the streets without any sense of shame. Everyone of them had in
his hand a scourger, made of leather thongs, and with tears and
groans they lashed themselves on their backs till the blood ran."

Very likely some of those early ecclesiastics who scourged themselves free of temptation, and won Heaven by the penal process, were
men of devout mind and pious life. At the same time it is certain
that the highest form of self-control is that of the will compelling
itself to an attitude of penitance. The chastisement of the body

cannot encourage repentance, for if the virtue lies in the endurance of pain, the penitent will aggravate his torture independently of his sins, and the more gratuitous the punishment the greater the glory.

In more modern times the Moycas, one of the tribes of New Granada, had the power of corporally chastising their spouses. General Quesada one day happened to call upon the chief of some village, whom he found writhing under the rods of all his nine wives. The explanation given was that he had got drunk with some Spaniards the night before, his wives had carried him to bed in order that he might sleep off the fumes of the liquors he had imbibed and in the morning awoke him to undergo punishment.

In Delowe's "Memorials of Human Superstition," there is the following curious tale about the fathers of St. Lazare in Paris. "Their establishment (that of the fathers) was a kind of banking-house, at which a cheque payable in blows was cashed for the bearer. Many parents or guardians availed themselves of this convenience in favour of refractory sons or pupils. Young people were sometimes clever enough to delude someone into the delivery of the sealed cheque for a thrashing, which was always made payable to bearer, notwithstanding all his protestations. Even ladies took revenge on faithless lovers by sending them with notes to the good fathers of St. Lazare, and the victims of the jest took care not to complain of the treatment they received lest they should be laughed at by the public.

This seminary at last became a terror of Paris. The fathers of St. Lazare lent their hands to such criminal dealings as occurred frequently in private lunatic asylums in England, and the Government suppressed the institution."

The rod has been in use in Courts. Catherine de Medicis, Queen of France, frequently laid her ladies of honour across her knees in order that she might herself punish them if they offended her, and until very recently a very similar state of things existed in St. Petersburg. In that pile-built city on the banks of the Neva, indeed, the rod is liberally in use behind the scenes. The ballet-girls not only in St. Petersburg but in the other cities of Russia, are conveyed every evening from a kind of seminary to the theatre, in a large closed conveyance, and should they not have the discretion to behave themselves, they have the stick for their supper on their return from the opera house or the theatre.

As our object is more the discussion of one particular branch of corporal discipline, we must henceforth endeavour to confine ourselves to the consideration of that branch—that which treats of corporal punishment as it is administered at this hour even in high-class ladies boarding-schools or "seminaries," as I believe their proprietresses prefer their establishments to be styled.

CHAPTER II.

IS IT RIGHT OR WRONG?

RIGHT say the mistresses; wrong say the girls. Who shall decide where women disagree? This is just the question which we shall endeavour to discuss but not to decide. Not being a lady we have neither been subjected to the form of punishment upon which we are writing, nor have we ever been concerned in the infliction of it. When a boy at school we have, however, had several experiences of this particular branch of the science of flagellation And, of course a boy could endure double or treble the amount of punishment that a girl of the same age could bear.

We shall not so much aim at forming a decided conclusion of our own on this matter, as, by publishing the experiences of ladies under the rod, our readers will have ample opportunity of forming half a dozen if they feel so inclined.

We recently asked the opinion of a young lady—herself intended for the scholastic profession—who has been whipped at various schools, both publicly and privately, at least a score times, on the merits of the old-fashioned whipping as applied to girls at the present day. She replied thus:—

" Although almost too young to offer an opinion, yet from what I have seen, I would not whip my pupils except as a last resort; still I would never take a pupil unless the matter was left entirely to my judgment. Other means failing after due warning, I would, without hesitation, smack or birch bad girls."

A lady of large experience in the tuition of children and grown-up girls, writes to us:—

"I may as well inform you at once that I am decidedly in favour of whipping as the best, and in many cases only means of enforcing discipline with children, and I make no distinction between boys and girls."

For ourselves, we think with the first-quoted lady, that it is not well to use the rod save as a last resort, and then, if every other means have failed, we would without scruple apply the forcible argument of personal chastisement.

Leaving for a time the question of whether flogging is justifiable or otherwise, we will now give the experience of the young lady from whom we have already quoted, on the occasion of her first whipping. We should mention that the offence for which this punishment was inflicted was wilful idleness and neglect of lessons, she having been several times previously cautioned for inattention to her duties. At length one day, her lessons having been culpably neglected, the governess of her class made a report to the mistress of the school, with whom the young lady—then about twelve years of age—immediately afterwards had a private interview. We take up the narrative from the point following the declaration of the culprit's sentence in the lady's own words:—

"She rose and came to the door, while I burst out crying, and threw myself on the floor. A fit of passion was upon me, but Miss —— deliberately stooped, and lifted me to my feet, saying, as she did so, 'Depend upon it, madam, you shall have a good whipping for this.' She half led, half carried me to her chair, seated herself, and, to my dismay, laid me face downwards across her knee. Perhaps I might have resisted, but my feet were off the floor before I knew what she was doing, for I had never been so punished before. I felt that it was all over with me, for it is perhaps the most helpless attitude in which a girl can be placed. Oh! the dreadful minute that preceded the punishment! I struggled and cried. 'Lie still, miss, will you?' said Miss ——; 'I shall keep you just as you are until you do.' 'Oh, ma'am!' I cried, 'let me get up; do, please Miss ——. I will never be so naughty again. Do let me go this time!' 'I will not,' was the reply. 'I never forgive such naughtiness. A great girl like you should be ashamed of such conduct. But perhaps, miss, the pain and disgrace of being whipped will make you behave yourself in future—at least I must try it. Not a word, miss. I will whip you well!' All impediments having been removed, settling me firmly on her knees, with right good will she began smacking my bare flesh with a short birch-rod which had been lying on the table beside her. . . . . My passion and rebellion gave way, but not all at once. It smarted dreadfully. I screamed with pain, writhed, and threw up my slippered feet again and again. I think I actually shouted for help. But the more I struggled the harder she flogged me, but so deliberately that she evidently kept her temper. 'Oh, don't, ma'am!' I cried; 'don't!'—Smack, swish, swish! 'Oh, dear! Oh, please!'—Swish; 'Do forgive me!'—Wish, smack, swish! 'Miss ——! oh, it's dreadful! Don't, don't!'—Swish, swish! 'Oh, dear! oh, dear! Oh, don't whip me any more!' Miss —— stopped the punishment for a moment. 'But I must, miss. It is painful for me to punish you, but your conduct deserves nothing else, you naughty girl. Will you learn your lessons, miss?'—Wish, wish! 'I have not done yet, and I will whip you well. Take your foot down this moment!'—Swish, swish! twig, twig! 'Will you behave yourself in future, miss?'—Wish, wish! 'I cannot bear it, Miss ——; I cannot, indeed. I will be good, I will! Oh, do give over!' 'Now, madam, this is additional for your disobedience in running to the door:—One, two, three, four, five, six! Then let that be a warning to you, miss, to behave yourself, and be diligent.'"

The result of this punishment was that the young girl who suffered it was never again whipped for that offence, and that it had a beneficial effect upon her she herself confesses. A whipping inflicted like this, at an early age, and when absolutely necessary, would, we think, frequently obviate the necessity for adopting such a course when the culprit has arrived at an age when such a punishment is, to say the least, most unseemly.

CHAPTER III.

ONE METHOD.

THERE are various methods of inflicting capital punishment in ladies' schools. A description of that most generally used will be gleaned from the following, from the pen of an accomplished lady who has studied the subject of school discipline in all its bearings :—

"*Some Account of a Whipping School.*

"I may state that I have been to several schools. both in England and France, but feel that I am not competent to give a good description of any of them. Although I have been often whipped, and sometimes very severely, I do not disapprove of such punishment when used with judgment, and when its application is made the exception and not the rule. I never received a whipping that I did not well deserve, and I felt so at the time of infliction. But while I myself was never punished undeservedly, I have known some who were, and that is the great danger of the method.

"The last school but one to which I went is, or was, kept by Madame A———. There punishments were often the most severe and the most shameful I have ever seen, although they were never given unjustly; and I must say, in justice to Madame A———, that forty-three naughtier girls could hardly be found. Their ages were from thirteen to nineteen, one or two being near twenty ; but all alike were liable to be whipped in nursery fashion for any serious naughtiness. Some of the girls were of very high families, and many were very troublesome girls, sent there as much for reformation as for a finishing education.

"I need not attempt to describe Madame A———; let me state, however, that there was something indescribably commanding in her look and manner, especially on certain occasions. Dreadfully severe as she was in her 'dernier ressort,' as she termed it, she was very lenient with respect to ordinary girlish offences. But for falsehood, pilfering, gross disobedience, indelicacy and impertinence, generally after one fair warning, which was publicly given and plainly expressed, a most severe whipping was certain to follow the first repetition.

"I have said that her punishments were the most shameful I ever saw, and generally this is true, for the reason that she often whipped young ladies before all their companions; her method and arrangements being such as to render the shame of a whipping as dreadful as the pain. Near the middle of the schoolroom, just before her desk, was a raised platform half a yard high, and large enough for four or five people to stand upon. When it became necessary to resort to extreme measures, Madame used to place a strong heavy chair on the platform, and then call up miss or mademoiselle, as the case might be.

"'Get up here, miss. Turn round and face your schoolfellows. Young ladies, sit round on your seats and look this way, if you please.' I need not say that all her orders were obeyed. She then produced from a drawer in her desk a stout elastic birch rod, which she handed to the blushing, trembling girl. 'Take this in your hand, miss. Hold it up so, if you please.' Madame then would point out the naughtiness of her offence, and remind her of the warnings she had had, speak to the others of the example, shame, and pain, and sometimes she would allow miss to return to her seat, but if not, madam ascended the platform, seated herself in the chair, and——* * * * * *

"The details, when ladies relate them, are only suitable for the ears of ladies.

"This was Madame A———'s 'dernier ressort'—a punishment not easily forgotten. She sometimes whipped in private, and also in presence of a select few, but she never adopted the method so common on the Continent, viz., that of removing the whole of the offender's garments, and strapping her down. Her whippings, if severe, were motherly.

"Madame A——— never whipped me but twice—severely only once, and that was in private, and any one would say that I richly deserved it. It was the only time I ever treated her badly. I have very good talent for drawing, and during the holidays I had been naughty enough to execute a finished water colour miniture drawing representing 'Madame A. giving the *dernier ressort* to a grown-up pupil. One of the governesses happened to search my desk (which she had no authority to do), and gave what she found to Madame A. The latter threw the drawing into her bureau, merely telling me to go to her boudoir and wait for her. She dismissed the governess on the spot for her dishonourable conduct; then coming to the boudoir, she gave me what I deserved.

"Had Madame known all, no doubt I should have suffered even more, for the drawing she took was not the finished one, but only a tracing of it touched up."

CHAPTER IV.

ANOTHER METHOD.

ANOTHER method of inflicting the punishment of the birch is by the "Horsing" process, which the following account, written by a lady some years ago, will perhaps explain :—

"When an offence of sufficient magnitude occurs, the culprit enters it in the book herself, and carries the report to the lady-superintendent, who writes in it the amount of punishment. For the first offence the delinquent is prepared for punishment, but generally pardoned. For the second she is whipped privately. For all subsequent delinquencies the punishment takes place in the schoolroom, and in addition to the pain it inflicts, it costs in money about 1s. in fees. This is the system :—1st. She (the culprit) proceeds to the housekeeper to procure the rod; she pays 2d. for the use of it. 2nd. She has then to be partly undressed by the maid, and this costs 2d. 3rd. The culprit has then to walk barefoot to another part of the house to be robed for punishment, a peculiar dress being used to add to the disgrace. It is a long linen blouse, short cotton socks, and list slippers. The young lady thus dressed now proceeds to the drawing-room to be exhibited to the lady-superintendent. Having been approved, she is then conducted to the schoolroom, where she has to pay 6d. to the governess who inflicts the punishment awarded. A wooden horse, covered with soft leather, is the medium of castigation. The culprit subsequently thanks the governess, kisses the rod, thanks the superintendent, and retires to her own room, to appear no more until prayer time the next morning. The ceremony has more effect than the punishment. Young ladies are, in all other respects, tenderly cared for. Even the horse has a soft cushion The soft cushion, we are told, is borrowed from Holland, where, as a friend some years ago told us, they have whipping establishments, to which parents send out their children to be punished. It seems they do so in Edinburgh also, for young ladies are sent to this Scotch house to get their faults whipped out of them."

Another lady writes thus :—

"I and two other girls were one day with the housekeeper in an old lumber room, or garret, in the school in which I was then at in Paris. In a corner of the room we saw a dusty, mouldy-looking piece of furniture, and none of us knew what it was. The house-keeper, who had been in the school long before the present owner lived in it, said it was a whipping-stool (cheval) in use many years ago. She then showed us how it was used, and fastened one of us on it. It was covered with dark baize, with a rounded cushion on the top, and was fitted with straps and rings."

It will thus be seen that the process above described is very similar to that in vogue when we were boys at school, and which, indeed, is still used in some public schools.

CHAPTER V.

PERSONAL EXPERIENCES.

IT has been often remarked that personal experience is the truest criterion, and we therefore submit the following extracts from pub-lished and unpublished experiences, which will assist our readers in forming their own opinions on this matter. It must be remembered that in penning this paper we desire to give each side a fair hearing, being ourselves impartial listeners only.

The first extract is from a letter written by a young lady at school, and which was printed in the columns of a well-known magazine nearly three years ago. She says:—

" I am seventeen, and there are older girls here that I, but we are all subjected to the same punishment. I saw one girl get the rod not three months ago, whom I knew to be fully twenty years of age. Then, besides the shame, the pain of it is dreadful. I never felt any-thing like it in my life before I came here. Every stroke produces the most horrid, stinging feeling, and it is worse than all to feel it, and to know that all the girls are watching to see if you will betray the agony you are suffering. Would you not think, if you saw a grown-up young lady screaming and writhing, and begging for mercy as the rod came down with that horrible swish on her quiver-ing flesh, that she had done something far worse than a garotter? And what would you think if you heard that she was suffering for having made four or five mistakes in her German lesson? You know the shameful way in which a young lady is prepared for the birch-rod where it is used. Is it not shocking? I am sure you know ladies of my age who would rather die than be disgraced by a punishment so inexpressibly degrading and ignominious. But Mrs. —— uses her rod with such severity that the sense of the indignity itself is soon lost in the intolerable pain that makes one feel as if you would do or say anything rather than bear it for another moment."

Thus another :—

"There are over forty of us here—some eighteen or twenty years of age—and we are all whipped like children with a birch-rod whenever the lady thinks fit, and often for mere trifles. . . . There is hardly any other punishment here, and a week seldom passes that Mrs. —— does not use her rod. . . . . I have been whipped twice since my birthday (May, and the letter is dated June), once for talking in the dormitory, and once for boxing the ears of a little girl who provoked me very much. For the last offence I got twenty strokes of a new birch-rod, and had to beg the girl's pardon on my knees before I was allowed to re-arrange my clothing. . . . I saw one public whipping since I came here, and I think I would rather die than bear it. . . . . Another girl was whipped and expelled shortly before I came for attempting to escape. She was birched till the blood ran down her limbs, and was handed into a cab the moment her clothes were replaced."

In one instance a gentleman wrote to the lady principal of a school, requesting a prospectus and particulars as to the mode of punishment adopted by her to her pupils. The following is an extract from her letter in reply.

"Discipline is enforced solely by the use of the birch rod; it is judiciously administered with the full consent of the parents. The only difference between older and younger pupils is that the latter have fewer strokes than the former; its average frequency would probably be weekly, and for grave offences about a dozen. The mode of infliction is simple. Either on rising from or immediately before retiring to rest, the delinquent is laid along a form—if resistance is offered a broad strap is passed round the waist and form—the night-dress is then raised above the waist and the birch is well applied."

The gentleman did not send his daughter to this school.

Quite a new phase of the subject is opened up by the letter of a young lady from which we extract the following:

" Sir,—I think you will find that the corporal correction of girls is much more practised at home than at public schools. We were all at schools where no personal chastisement of any description was in use, but mamma always maintained her parental authority over daughters with the rod so long as they remained unmarried. Some of us indeed have not been whipped for years, but still we know that she would whip us if she thought we deserved it. We do not think much of the disgrace when she does it, and perhaps no one in the house knows of it being done, but the pain is sometimes dreadful—I say sometimes, for she always prides herself on suiting the infliction to the offence. The last time I experienced it—I won't say how old I was—I went out when mamma had told me to remain in, and hearing her carriage returning I ran in hastily through a side door and unfortunately destroyed an article of value. I stoutly denied all about it, but it was traced to me and I was whipped. The pain was so sharp that after about ten strokes I sprang up and cried out that I could bear it no longer, but she tied me down and applied the birch again till I struggled and roared like a child of five. Do you think that even for disobedience and falsehood a grown girl should be put to such frightful pain?"

Such a letter certainly leads one to believe that corporal punishment is more severe when practised at home than when inflicted at school. Without doubt the young lady in question was deserving of punishment in some shape, and dozens of methods might have been resorted to other than the one actually used. The good effect of punishment of any kind is only to be secured by its judicious application, and systematic or habitual severity of correction cannot fail to achieve exactly the opposite result to the one desired.

The next is a case in which ill-timed and unnecessary severity appears to have been used. The letter is written by one, and in the name of three young ladies at the same seminary together.

"I will tell you what happened to us three girls last Monday week. We all three had been set an imposition, and were sent upstairs to do it. . . . The other young ladies were gone for a walk, so we got a pack of cards, and joined in a game which took up our attention so much that we forgot how the time was going, and Miss —— found us with the cards in our hands. Not a stroke of the imposition was done. Miss —— was in a dreadful rage, and ordered us off to bed at once. We thought that was all, but she soon came in herself with the junior governess, and the housemaid with her, and we were each in turn made to lie across the foot of one of the beds, when the junior governess held our hands and arms, and pressed on our shoulders, and the servant held our feet, while Miss —— inflicted a terrible flogging on the back and thighs with a horrible rod."

Of course the three girls were very much in the wrong! not so much perhaps in neglecting their impositions as in practising with the cards. Had we been in the place of the mistress mentioned above we should ourselves no doubt have inflicted a severe punishment, and even if it had been a corporal one, we are quite certain that we should not have gone to such an unwarrantable length as did the lady mentioned by our correspondents.

CHAPTER VI.

THE following extract shows a refinement of cruelty which we should not have thought was in vogue in England, although we might have believed it of any other country. Truly there are "more things in heaven and earth than are dreamt of in our philosophy":—

"Seven times have I suffered the birch in two years, and some of the girls have had it as often in six months. The pain is something terrible, to say nothing of the disgrace. The punishment takes place in Miss ——'s dressing-room, where there is a large ottoman covered with chintz, the pattern of which I shall remember as long as I live, for while lying face downwards upon it, I have suffered most exquisite pain and torture. To this ottoman are attached straps to confine the waist and hands, so that when lying along the ottoman bound in this way we are completely helpless."

We think we cannot do better than conclude with a quotation from a very sensible and able article on this subject, but which, it must be remembered, is written entirely from one standpoint—that of " pain and disgust " (we quote the writer's own words) at the system of birching. He says—

" Some thirty years ago, when flogging in the army and navy was the rule, public opinion spoke loudly against it, and was met by the assertion of numerous officers that its abolition would prove the ruin of our defensive forces. But public opinion prevailed. The ' cat-o'-nine-tails' was abolished, and what are the two services now? Let the history of the Crimean War, the expedition to the Baltic under Sir Charles Napier, the suppression of the Indian Mutiny, in which both services took part, speak for the benefit of the new system. And small though its number may be in comparison with the armies of the Continent, the admirable efficiency of the English army has drawn forth the following trite remark from a foreign general: ' It is fortunate that they are not more numerous.' As for our navy, it is acknowledged to be the most efficient in the world, and the whole machinery is perfected without the aid of flogging. Why then is it necessary that in young ladies' schools the birch, the ferula, and the riding-whip should still be necessary? The question admits of but one answer—that the teachers lack tact of ruling by love, and appeal to terror only as the means of preserving their sovereignty. We can understand a certain amount of correction being necessary to young children, but even then only under certain circumstances; and we maintain that if a teacher possesses the proper capacity for her position, she will easily preserve her authority among her older pupils without having recourse to weapons that leave red marks behind, or require kid gloves to ' prevent the abrasion of the skin.' We see no reason why the principal of a seminary should not look upon her pupils as a family committed to her charge, nor why her pupils should not look up to her as they would to a kind and affectionate mother. It is a matter of tact and management only. The parents of the young ladies themselves have much to answer for when they consent to so vile a punishment being inflicted. Does it never occur to them that they are making their daughters suffer torture for their own mismanagement of them during their younger days—that they have themselves sown the seeds of passion and indolence by the over-indulgence of their childish tempers—that while they have laughed at the amusing petulence of an infant, they have forgotten that that petulence would grow stronger as the child increased in years? Let them reflect. Now as to the legality of the punishment. Some years back a fiction was prevalent that a man could chastise his wife with a cane no thicker than his finger. Such an absurdity only needed a magisterial case to prove the contrary; and we unhesitatingly assert that should a case of the birch be brought before a magistrate, the production of the parent's written consent for the punishment would not only prove insufficient for the protection of the principal of the school, but would subject the parents to a severe rebuke for their cruelty. Medical testimony is not wanting as to its pernicious effects on the constitution, but obvious reasons prevent us from entering into this branch of the question. We are well aware that in all large or small assemblies, whether of pupils or not, there are certain to be found some intractable characters—some on whom all kindness, all efforts seem to be thrown away, but we have invariably found, and writers whose footsteps we desire to follow at a respectful distance, acknowledge that there is no heart so hard but has a soft spot in it, and if the teacher has not the ability to find it, she has at least this alternative—she can get rid of the intractable one, and she may rely that for every unruly pupil she expels she will secure two good ones in return Let us trust that the good feeling of teachers will found on our remarks some better system that will shortly send Queen Birch to the same old curiosity shop to which the cat with many tails has been consigned; that parents who really love their daughters will be careful to see that their children are placed in schools where principals do not depend upon the birch as a means of enforcing discipline."

www.ingramcontent.com/pod-product-compliance
Lightning Source LLC
Chambersburg PA
CBHW081308040426
42452CB00014B/2699